POCKET PORTFOLIO®
–Number Seven–

CRATER LAKE

NATIONAL PARK

including
DEEP BLUE WILDERNESS
by
RON WARFIELD

SIERRA PRESS
Mariposa, CA

ISBN 0-939365-60-X

PRODUCTION CREDITS

Series Editor-in-Chief: Jeff Nicholas
Book Design: Jeff Nicholas
Essay and Captions: Ron Warfield
Editor: Nicky Leach
Photo Editor: Jeff Nicholas
Production Assistant: Laura Bucknall
Printing coordination: TWP America, Inc.

Front Cover: Wizard Island and Mount Scott, sunrise. JEFF GNASS.
Frontispiece: Mountain hemlocks on the caldera's rim frame
        Wizard Island, winter. JON GNASS.
Title Page: Crater Lake, early morning. STEVE TERRILL.
Back Cover: Llao Rock and Wizard Island, winter evening.
        STEVE TERRILL.

COLLECT THE ENTIRE POCKET PORTFOLIO® SERIES

No. 1—ARCHES & CANYONLANDS NATIONAL PARKS
No. 2—GRAND CANYON NATIONAL PARK
No. 3—MOUNT ST. HELENS NATIONAL VOLCANIC
        MONUMENT
No. 4—YOSEMITE NATIONAL PARK
No. 5—DEATH VALLEY NATIONAL PARK
No. 6—SEQUOIA & KINGS CANYON NATIONAL PARKS
No. 7—CRATER LAKE NATIONAL PARK
No. 8—YELLOWSTONE NATIONAL PARK
No. 9—COLUMBIA RIVER GORGE NATIONAL SCENIC AREA
No. 10—OLYMPIC NATIONAL PARK
No. 11—MOUNT RAINIER NATIONAL PARK
No. 12—GLACIER NATIONAL PARK

The publishers would like to take this opportunity to express our
appreciation to the photographers who made their imagery
available for review during the editing of this title. On behalf of
those who will view this book—Thank You!

If you would like to receive a complimentary
catalog of our publications,
please call: **(800) 745-2631**
e-mail: siepress@yosemite.net
or write: **SIERRA PRESS**
4988 Gold Leaf Drive, Mariposa, CA 95338

SIERRA PRESS

Sunrise from Discovery Point.

GARY BRAASCH

At Crater Lake, creation stares us squarely in the face. Crater Lake is immense. Arguably the most beautiful lake in the world, it rests in a textbook example of a caldera, a large volcanic collapse basin. The lake is an unexpected gem in the vast Cascade Range volcanic landscape extending from California's Lassen Peak to British Columbia's Mount Garibaldi. The caldera rim looms, on average, 1,500 feet above the surface of the 1,932-foot deep lake. An idea of the lake's depth can be had by noting that as much of the caldera is hidden below the lake surface as projects above it. Now recovered from total devastation as a result of the climactic eruptions of Mount Mazama, coniferous forests and associated animal species soften the approach to the scarred flanks of the old volcano. The grotesque wind-sculpted forms of whitebark pines cling to the caldera rim, defying hundreds of harsh seasons.

DEEP BLUE WILDERNESS

Essay by Ron Warfield

HIDDEN IN ITS SUBLIME SETTING UNTIL THE FINAL MOMENT, Crater Lake bursts into one's consciousness in full-blown glory upon first sight. Regardless of what people expect upon arrival at the rim of the caldera, they react in the same way. Thousands of well travelled place-baggers stop in their tracks, cease their conversations about "more important stuff," and just gape.

After exhaling whatever breath remains at this 7,000-foot elevation, gasps of amazement usually blend into textbook looks of surprise. It's the dinosaur brain trying to devour the immense scene in one impossible gulp. Everyone just stands there, joins with the silence, and stares into the abyss. Its BIG! And its BLUE...the most indescribable blue.

Crater Lake looks blue, even on cloudy days, because of its great clarity and depth, and because of the way that sunlight penetrates the water. When sunlight enters, pure water molecules act as tiny prisms to scatter the light and break up the different light wavelengths into spectral colors. Reds and yellows are absorbed very close to the water's surface. Greens are absorbed within only a few meters of water (hence the greenish tint around the edge of the lake as most of the light is reflected back upward from the lake bed).

At great depth, only blues and indigos of the spectrum remain to be continually scattered by the water molecules. Some blue is eventually redirected into our eyes. The more direct the sunlight, the more intense the impression of blueness. Of course, the water itself is transparent, without color.

On a bright sunny day, many observers suppose that the lake is blue because it reflects the blue sky. And to some extent, wave action creates a slight mirror effect on the water's surface, enhancing its blueness. At this elevation, sunlight reaches the lake without passing through too much hazy air, so it penetrates deeper into this transparent water than into any other lake on Earth.

It's a fragile purity, which could easily be disturbed by human activities. Since no streams flush the lake, it's practically a closed system. So woe unto us if we put anything into the water of the bluest of all lakes.

This blue sea of silence draws us into its spell and forever changes the way we view ourselves as we try to understand the awesome forces that created this famous place. We come away with respect for the greater cosmos when we realize that we cannot improve upon it. Humbled by this knowledge, we feel a commitment to protect the integrity of such places. The noise of civilization sometimes needs the reassurance of silence to keep itself on track. By preserving the lake, we enhance our humanity. We need to leave Crater Lake just the way it is, so that it may continue to inspire us.

The native peoples living in the Klamath Marshes were witnesses to the final spasms of Mount Mazama. Today, though their voices are stilled and the mountain now sleeps, the climactic eruption lives on in the legends of Klamath Tribes. The stories of Llao and Skell, although told by people who have a different cosmology, seem prophetic. Skell, Chief of the Above World, who lived on the top of Mount Shasta, beheaded Llao, Chief of the Below World, who lived beneath Mount Mazama. The two Chiefs hurled rocks over the heads of the people until Skell finally drove Llao back underground in a cataclysmic battle. These are not figments of native imagination but eyewitness accounts of the final days of the mountain that used to be. Their stories awaken new insights as new peoples come to ponder the origins of the lake, its setting, and its meaning in the greater order of things.

Opposite: Mount Scott and Crater Lake, dawn. JON GNASS.

Skell Channel between Wizard Island and the shoreline of the caldera.   WILLARD CLAY

Cloud reflected in Crater Lake.

GARY BRAASCH

Crater Lake is the deepest lake in the United States and the seventh deepest in the world. The famous blue color of the water results from its depth and transparency: using an eight-inch Secchi disc, researchers have recorded a world-record 142-foot-clarity reading (43.3 meters). With no inlets or outlets, only rainfall and snowmelt feed the lake. Input nearly balances seepage and evaporation, so that lake surface level fluctuates only one to four feet per year. Although Crater Lake has no native fish, rainbow trout and kokanee salmon were introduced as sport fish in the early 1900s. These fish have significantly altered the zooplankton community in the lake. Researchers continue to monitor the relationships among the lake and climate, physical and chemical characteristics, and ecology in an effort to preserve the pristine nature of Crater Lake.

Dramatic late-afternoon light on the lake.

RON WARFIELD

Long before Crater Lake National Park was established on May 22, 1902, word of the incredible blueness of the lake was known far and wide. Klamath and other Indian tribes had revered the lake for generations, then gold prospectors John Wesley Hillman, Henry Klippel, and Isaac Skeeters "discovered" the lake in 1853 and named it Deep Blue Lake. William Gladstone Steel became preoccupied with Crater Lake in 1870 after reading about the lake in a newspaper article wrapped around his school lunch. When he finally saw the lake in 1885, Steel was hooked: He devoted his life to helping establish Crater Lake National Park and became its second manager. He participated in scientific surveys, touted the lake's wonders, and named many caldera landmarks, including Wizard Island, Llao Rock, and Skell Head. Steel established Crater Lake Lodge in 1915 and oversaw completion of Rim Drive in 1918. Today's visitors can now enjoy their excursion in comfort while minimizing their impact upon the unique values of this natural system.

Storm clouds above Hillman Peak, sunset.

LARRY ULRICH

RACING DOWN THE CLEETWOOD COVE TRAIL to catch the day's first boat tour, I'm struck by the absolute stillness of the scene. Phantom Ship has melded into the face of Dutton Cliff. Wizard Island cone has become a perfect reflection of itself in Llao's transparent mirror. Upon the lake, our boat seems suspended in reflections while my mind spirals as it tries to keep reality from merging with facsimile. With resonant clouds below every bit as intense as real clouds overhead, I content myself with just gazing upon the reflection. Caldera rim features form a new closer horizon.

The reflective spell breaks as soon as I step onto the rubbly lava flow at the base of the Wizard Island cinder cone. I'm standing within the remains of Mount Mazama, a 420-thousand year old composite volcano. Crater Lake partly fills the caldera which formed in the climactic eruptions of Mount Mazama about 7,700 years ago. This eruption vented more than 50 cubic kilometers of magma and spread pumice and ash over a large part of the Pacific Northwest. After the collapse, landslides widened the caldera and lava flows and domes erupted as lake waters collected during a period of 300 years. Wizard Island erupted as the lake finished filling, while Merriam Cone erupted underwater and remains completely submerged. Volcanic activity has been quiet for nearly 4,250 years, allowing organic-rich muds to accumulate on submerged volcanic features. Standing here, in the midst of it all, I'm as excited as the geologists who unraveled the mysteries of the cataclysmic events that occurred here.

I remain at the water's edge, intrigued by the reflections and seemingly enhanced transparency. Peering into the limpid mirror, I feel a cold splash and hear bubbles before realizing, with embarrassment, that my face has broken the surface. Shaking the cold water from my face, I notice a dark green band in the depths near the shoreline. Deep sunlight penetration of the transparent water permits thick moss carpets to flourish on the lake bottom at depths of 18 to 130 meters—deeper than in any other lake. Though volcanic eruptions paused several millennia ago, geothermal heat still enters the caldera beneath the lake. Recent research has revealed vivid yellow-orange mats of bacteria growing in water 35 degrees warmer than the surrounding lake water.

Departing Wizard Island, we once more ride on the surface of a magic mirror. Approaching the lava flow cliff of the Palisades, the boat slows to greet the "Old Man of the Lake," an upright floating log, which was deposited in Crater Lake by an avalanche. Over the decades, the "Old Man" has enjoyed many reflections while wandering around the lake pushed by wind currents. I envy him. He remains afloat on the ethereal deep blue lake, but I can spend only fleeting moments on its sapphire, mirrored surface.

Phantom Ship projects 160 feet above the mirror-perfect reflection of Dutton Cliff. Sunset silhouettes the 300-foot-long island in shimmering incandescence when viewed from Kerr Notch or Sentinel Rock. Sun Notch and Garfield Peak Trails offer equally stunning views of Phantom Ship at sunrise. Other viewpoints around the caldera rim offer sporadic glimpses of the tiny island, giving rise to the name—Phantom Ship. Boat tours circle the island daily in summer, providing close-up views. Morning tours provide more consistent opportunity for reflections of the ship's stony sails. Phantom Ship, composed of volcanic ejecta and andesite lava flows, contains the oldest rocks within the caldera. These lavas are part of the 400,000-year-old Phantom Cone, an early volcanic precursor to Mount Mazama. Phantom Cone and Phantom Ship were uncovered at the base of Dutton Cliff when Mount Mazama collapsed to form the Crater Lake caldera.

Opposite: Phantom Ship. JEFF GNASS.

Wizard Island, so named because of its resemblance to a medieval wizard's hat, projects 763 feet above the surface of Crater Lake. The symmetrical cone dominates the view from the Watchman. Wizard Island is a classic cinder cone, formed after the collapse of Mount Mazama. Renewed volcanic activity following the climactic eruption formed the central platform, Wizard Island, and Merriam Cone—andesitic volcanic features projecting from the caldera floor. Recent research indicates that the lower portion of Wizard Island erupted underwater, but that the central platform was erupted earlier, and was then submerged by the rising waters of Crater Lake. Merriam Cone may also have erupted underwater as the lake level rose. Wizard Island cone then continued to grow above the present lake surface. Boat tourists may disembark at the island and climb the steep 1.5-mile trail to the 300-foot-wide summit crater or visit shallow pools formed in blocky lava flows along the western shore.

Wizard Island, sunrise.

STEVE TERRILL

Mountain hemlocks and Fumarole Bay, Wizard Island.

JEFF GNASS

Trunk of whitebark pine on the rim of Crater Lake.

LARRY ULRICH

Snowpack and weather permitting, most visitors first see the lake from Rim Village, where Sinnott Memorial Overlook offers an unobstructed panorama of the entire caldera. A mountain-top view from Garfield Peak can be had from a vantage point 1,900 feet above the blue lake surface—roughly the same height above the water as the lake bottom is below the surface. One mile from Rim Village, Discovery Point provides the same rich sunrise view seen by three prospectors in 1853. Nearly four miles from Rim Village, the Watchman Overlook frames a spectacular view of Wizard Island between the cluster of sharp spires forming Hillman Peak and the craggy face of the Watchman. Visitors approaching from the north gain their first lake view at North Junction, where battered whitebark pines mark the caldera rim. The impressive 1,200-foot-face of sheer Llao Rock looms to the left of the overlook.

Garfield Peak, The Watchman, and Hillman Peak, winter.

BRUCE JACKSON/Jon Gnass Photo Images

THERE ARE TWO SEASONS HERE: WINTER AND AUGUST. Or so it seems. Winter storms can begin as early as late-August and, in many years, spring snowstorms continue into June. Visitors arriving from lower elevations and warmer climes are surprised to find snowbanks lingering through the summer season in places like the Watchman, Llao Rock, and Cloudcap. It's a harsh environment, but hardy plants soften the landscape around the caldera. Only woody shrubs and trees, which have extensive root systems to gather water and nutrients efficiently, tough out heavy snowpacks and desiccating winds to project more than a few inches above the ground surface. Icy blasts of winter nip buds from the windward sides of gnarly whitebark pines around the rim, giving them a distinct flagged appearance. Rime ice wraps mountain hemlocks in ghostlike shrouds. The pines and hemlocks respond to wind and weight by bending into grotesque shapes. Shasta red firs grow rigidly, but often lose their single brittle tops to battering winds, giving them a candelabra appearance. On exposed ridges and higher summits, ice crystals carried in storm winds grind bark from ancient trees, leaving the underlying wood to sun-bleach to silver as decades pass. If you look carefully, you'll see that trees atop Cloudcap seem to grow in parallel rows. The climactic eruption of Mount Mazama left dunes of pumice over this landscape. Whitebark pines have colonized the dune tops, but slow-melting snowbanks and shifting pumice among the dunes have retarded the development of a continuous cover. These tortured (*krummholz*) trees have twisted limbs and broken trunks—the result of countless wind-torn winters.

Each spring, bright yellow swirls of conifer pollen coat the lake surface. Conifers take advantage of the short summer season to produce the next generation. Most herbaceous plants growing near Crater Lake spring from perennial root systems and keep their crowns in tight clumps that remain close to ground level in order to conserve moisture and avoid battering winds. The few perennial sedges and herbs that have managed to colonize areas such as the Pumice Desert contend not only with lack of surface water and nutrients but also with continual disturbance of the soil surface by needle ice. Annual plants germinate, grow quickly, flower, and set seed at a breakneck pace to get their reproductive job done in the few short weeks, from snowmelt to first killing frost.

By late August, summer is already over. Flashes of burgundy and scarlet from Newberry fleeceflower in higher-elevation pumice flats herald the change of season. Now is the time to watch chipmunks, golden-mantled ground squirrels, yellow-bellied marmots, and pikas gather seeds and dried vegetation for their winter survival. Raucous Clark's nutcrackers pry open tightly closed whitebark pine cones and stash the seeds for later snacking. Seeds not relocated as food become the next generation of pines. By October, winter's blustery storms wrap the lake once more in a cold white blanket of silence.

Pinnacles of buff-colored pumice and gray scoria project along the canyon walls of Sand, Wheeler, and Munson Creeks. Their hollow spires are evidence of the lifeless landscape punctuated by fumaroles left in the wake of Mount Mazama's climactic eruption. As the 200-foot-deep blanket of seething pumice and scoria cooled, vertical cracks penetrated deep into the loosely-bonded mass. Then creek waters cut steep-walled V-shaped canyons. Water and wind have widened the canyons leaving the erosion resistant, cemented fumarole walls to form colonnades of turrets and gargoyles. Forests of mountain hemlock, subalpine fir, and lodgepole pine have regained a foothold, their spirelike forms echoing the pinnacles in the rock. Winds occasionally sweep up volumes of loose volcanic ash, forming dust clouds that give a surrealistic cast to the scene.

Opposite: Pumice pinnacles near Wheeler Creek. ADAM BACHER.

Rock faces seem at first glance to be the harshest of environments, but closer inspection yields a myriad of tiny niches for many unique and hardy plants. Garfield Peak, Mount Scott, and the Watchman Lookout Trails provide close-up views of sturdy Davidson's penstemons and dwarf hulseas. Moist areas along streams, especially near springs, harbor such gems as bog orchids, miterworts, and elephanthead pedicularis. Annie Creek Trail, near Mazama Campground, provides varied habitats where many streamside species grow. Castle Crest Wildflower Garden near Park Headquarters in Munson Valley delights flower lovers. Skyrocket gilia on the dry slopes attract rufous hummingbirds in July and August. Monkeyflowers and many other species grow in profusion as the snowbanks retreat. Newberry fleeceflowers and just a few herbaceous species, such as sulfur flowers and pussy paws, provide sparse groundcover in the Pumice Desert. This hostile but fragile environment is the result of extreme surface temperature fluctuations and a porous, nutrient-poor soil.

Lewis monkeyflower and seep-spring arnica, Kerr Valley.

LARRY ULRICH

The Pumice Desert, sunset.

JEFF GNASS

Staghorn lichen on mountain hemlocks deformed by heavy snows.

JEFF GNASS

Deep winter in the forest near the rim.   STEVE TERRILL

Whitebark pine near North Junction.   JEFF GNASS

The rich plant mosaic in Crater Lake National Park's 183,224 acres results from just seven millennia of regrowth following the destruction wrought by Mount Mazama's climactic eruptions. Nearly 600 plant species have re-emerged here, attesting to the resilience of ecosystems in the face of horrendous volcanic disturbance. Huge ponderosa pines and white firs dominate drier southern and northeastern lower slopes in the park. On wetter western slopes, Douglas-firs, sugar pines, and several true fir species dominate. Well adapted to poor soil conditions and extremes of temperature and moisture, lodgepole pines cover intermediate slopes. A mixture of mountain hemlocks and Shasta red firs grow in open clusters at higher elevations. Staghorn lichen gives a chartreuse patina to the normally reddish-brown, furrowed bark of these trees. Wind-shaped whitebark pines battle foul weather around the caldera rim and on exposed ridgetops. Montane meadows and streambanks are bordered by subalpine fir, Engelmann spruce, and the occasional black cottonwood and quaking aspen.

A profusion of herbaceous vegetation is scattered throughout the forests and the wetland areas in the lower western part of the park. Prodigious flows of water from Boundary Springs, the source of the Rogue River, support lush growths of mosses and yellow monkeyflowers. Thousand Springs, the largest spring complex in the park, supports more than 120 species of wet meadow plants, such as alpine shooting stars and bog orchids. Sphagnum Bog, fed by Crater Springs, is home to a variety of bog-dwelling flora, including some carnivorous species of bladderworts and sundews. Mats of floating sphagnum mosses growing over deep pools of cold water have surprised unwary hikers. Carpets of wildflowers in these wetland areas and Red Blanket Canyon reward visitors willing to hike far enough into the backcountry to view them. For the rest of us, the Castle Crest Wildflower Garden, Annie Creek Canyon, Godfrey Glen, and Vidae Falls areas offer colorful wildflower displays of Lewis monkeyflowers, monkshood, and arrowleaf groundsels.

Fireweed and arnica below Vidae Falls.

LARRY ULRICH

Rogue River Gorge near Union Creek (Rogue River National Forest).

STEVE TERRILL

GET UP! GET UP AND ONTO THE ROOF—WITH A SHOVEL!" shouted the park's Chief of Maintenance. It was four o'clock in the morning, Easter Sunday, 1983. Roofs were collapsing, so the Easter Bunny would have to wait.

That Crater Lake receives a lot of snow each winter is common knowledge. Indeed, Crater Lake holds the Oregon state record for deepest snowpack on the ground: 21 feet, set in 1983. We were there on that day—shovelling snow from the roofs of Crater Lake's historic structures.

The winter of 1982-1983 began normally, with some light snowfalls in late August and early September. The snowpack began to pile up in October, and then through the holidays it seemed to snow nearly every day, sometimes as much as a foot of snow, as storm after storm raced in from the southwest. When we could no longer see out of second-story windows because the snowpack had reached the eaves, we could still see light because snowplows continually rumbled past our front doors. By the end of March, snowplows had stacked snow on roadsides as high as a three-story building.

The lake remained indescribably blue, rimmed by the softest of white blankets. Cross-country skiers complained of "too much powder." Few ventured beyond Discovery Point, only a mile into the normally accessible 33-mile ski circuit of the rim.

On "warm" days between storms, local pre-schoolers would climb out of upstairs windows and assemble a tea party on the snowbank. Entertainment for the youngsters was provided by the ever-present antics of ravens, Clark's nutcrackers, gray jays, and Steller's jays. Watching children interact with the birds, I often wondered just who was entertaining whom.

Most park employees carried flashlights at night—not for route finding but for avoiding porcupines. Busy porcupines move slowly and are not the kind of boot scrapers with which you would want to dance toe to toe. Other mammals, such as elk and blacktail deer, generally avoided deep snows of winter by migrating to lowlands around the park. Sometimes a Cascades red fox or a coyote climbed down into the roadway and became stuck in the 30-foot rut, loping for miles in search of an exit from the white maze.

Snowplow drivers, the unsung heroes of winter at Crater Lake, keep snow from blocking access to Park Headquarters. But often, despite their most heroic efforts, the last three miles of roadway from Munson Valley to Rim Village is opened late in the day. In the winter of 1982-1983, Rim Village and a lake view were inaccessible for many weeks, unless you skied or snowshoed up the Raven Trail.

Those were the most enjoyable days to make the effort to ski to the caldera rim. Standing on the rim at such times overwhelmed me with the silent majesty of the place. Surrounded by winter's pristine wilderness, I could easily imagine being the first person ever to see this grand scene.

On days when ski tracks coursed toward Rim Village, ahead of my own intended route, I headed the other way, toward Sun Notch, for a taste of winter wilderness. An easy route in summer, it takes more than four times the effort in winter to catch a glimpse of the Phantom Ship. The hazard of breaking through a snow cornice near the edge is more than doubled. But, no matter. My heart leaped every time I saw this classic view. Sometimes it seems that rewards double if efforts to attain a goal require a bit of huff and puff.

From the top of 8,929-foot Mount Scott, a superb panorama takes in all that remains of vanished Mount Mazama and affords a unique aerial perspective on the caldera. The other conical Cascade stratovolcanoes, Mount McLoughlin and Mount Shasta, loom to the south-southwest, with Mount Shasta more than a hundred miles away. Alternating layers of thick lava flows and explosive ejecta form steep-sided stratovolcanoes. To the southwest lies Union Peak, the remains of an extinct composite volcano. Glaciation has removed most of its gently sloping flanks, leaving only an erosion-resistant central plug. The steeper Mount Thielsen pierces the northern horizon. Extensive glacial erosion has steepened its northern and eastern flanks and made it the "lightning rod of the Cascades." The white mounds of the Three Sisters stratovolcanoes cap the view 82 miles to the north. Mount Scott is the easternmost cone in the series of overlapping cones that formed the Mount Mazama volcano complex. The 2.5-mile trail to Mount Scott's summit climbs steeply through *krummholz* stands of whitebark pine.

Opposite: Mount Thielsen and Grotto Cove from Skell Head. LARRY ULRICH.

Cleetwood Cove provides the only trail access to the lake. A 1.1-mile trail descends in a steep, 720-foot zig-zag to the cove and boat dock. Cloudcap provides what feels like an almost aerial view of the lake and the slopes of Mount Scott. The imposing face of Redcloud Cliff testifies to the complex volcanic history of the caldera. Overlapping lava flows from one of the groups of volcanoes forming Mount Mazama make up its base. Explosive eruptions showered layers of pumice and welded tuff (where the pumice remelted near the explosive vent) atop older lava flows. Pumice Castle is the eroded remains of these pumice-fall deposits. Kerr Notch, resting in a U-shaped, glacially carved valley truncated by the collapse of Mount Mazama, frames a fine view of the Phantom Ship. Sun Notch rewards hikers with flowers and a superb view of the tiny island. Walk, don't run, the last 100 yards to the rim before gazing into the blue abyss.

The Pumice Castle and Redcloud Cliff.

WILLIAM NEILL

Mount Scott and moon from near Cleetwood Trail.

WILLARD CLAY

During the winter of 1985, nearly 99 percent of Crater Lake's surface froze.

RON WARFIELD

At this 7,000-foot elevation, winter grips the Crater Lake landscape for most of the year. Although snow could fall on any day of summer, winter storms usually begin in late-September and continue into June. An average of 530 inches of snow falls on the lake, adding nearly 70 inches of precipitation to the waters of the lake. The deepest snows on record in Oregon occurred at Crater Lake in April 1983, when snow fell to a depth of 21 feet. With all the snow, you might expect the lake surface to freeze every winter, but, in fact, it rarely ices over. The last time the lake surface froze completely was in 1949, although 1985 saw a 99 percent ice cover. The immense lake stores the sun's summer heat and usually retards ice formation throughout winter. In colder months the 38-degree Fahrenheit, intensely blue lake waters contrast sharply with the dazzling white snow. Cliff penstemons and spreading phlox splash color on the caldera walls as snowbanks recede in early summer.

Opposite: Moonrise at sunset, winter. DENNIS FLAHERTY.

FOR MORE INFORMATION

CRATER LAKE NATIONAL PARK
Crater Lake, OR 97604
(541) 594-2211

CRATER LAKE NATURAL HISTORY ASSOCIATION
P.O. Box 157
Crater Lake, OR 97604
(541) 594-2211 x498
e-mail address: crla_nha@nps.gov

**VISIT THE NATIONAL PARKS ON
THE INTERNET:** http://www.nps.gov

ACCOMMODATIONS

INSIDE THE PARK:
LODGING RESERVATIONS:
CRATER LAKE LODGE COMPANY
(541) 830-8700 (Reservations)
(541) 830-8514 (Fax)
(541) 594-2255 (Rim information)
e-mail address: info@crater-lake.com
On the Internet: www.crater-lake.com

OUTSIDE THE PARK:
KLAMATH COUNTY
CHAMBER OF COMMERCE
107 Plum Avenue
Klamath Falls, OR 97601
(541) 884-5193, (541) 884-5195 (Fax)
On the Internet:
www.cdsnet.net/Business/KlamathChamber

THE CHAMBER OF MEDFORD/JACKSON COUNTY
101 East 8th Street
Medford, OR 97501
(800) 469-6307, (541) 776-4808 (Fax)
On the Internet:
http://www.medfordchamber.com

ROSEBURG VISITOR & CONVENTION BUREAU
410 S.E. Spruce (P.O. Box 1262)
Roseburg, OR 97470
(800) 444-9584, (541) 673-7868 (Fax)

Clark's Nutcracker.   STEVE TERRILL